French

Key Stage 2
For ages 7-9

Practise & Learn

Published by CGP

Editors:
Lucy Loveluck
Matteo Orsini Jones
Holly Poynton

CD contributors:
Chris Dennett
Anne-Laure Kenny
Sam Norman

With thanks to Samantha Bensted, Florence Bonneau,
Sandrine Moyle and Jennifer Underwood for the proofreading.

ISBN: 978 1 84762 986 9

With thanks to Jan Greenway for the copyright research.

Printed by Elanders Ltd, Newcastle upon Tyne
Clipart from Corel®

Based on the classic CGP style created by Richard Parsons.

Contents

Hello!

Bonjour!

bonsoir good evening

bonne nuit good night

à bientôt see you soon

pas mal not bad

très bien very well

pas très bien not very well

Fill in the gaps below to make a phrase for each picture.

Remember!
'Bonne nuit' is what you'd say before going to bed — just like 'good night'.

b o n n e n u i t

B o n j o u r

p a s t r è s b i e n

a u r e v o i r

The characters below have been asked "Ça va?".
Read their replies and answer the questions below.

1 Who said that they are not bad? alfonse

2 Who said that they are very well? renée

3 Who said that they are well? claude

4 Who said that they are not very well? Gérard

Unscramble these French words.

b j r o o n u	l u s a t	r v u i e a o r
bonjour	salut	au revoir

Draw lines to match the French words to the English words.

bonjour

bonne nuit

salut

hi

hello

bonsoir

a bientôt

good evening

see you soon

good night

What is your name?

Comment t'appelles-tu?

Comment t'appelles-tu?
What is your name?

Je m'appelle Charlotte.
I am called Charlotte.

Il s'appelle Chompy.
He is called Chompy.

Elle s'appelle...
She is called...

Ils s'appellent...
They are called...

Remember!
'Elle' means 'she' and 'il' means 'he'.

Write the correct name from each pair of brackets below.

Il s'appelle (Sarah/William). → William

Elle s'appelle (Katherine/Jack). → ....

Il s'appelle (Olivia/Sanjay). → ....

Elle s'appelle (Emily/Connor). → ....

Colour the boxes that form a phrase in the same colour.

Comment	Je	m'	t'	appelle	appellent
Il	s'	s'	appelles-	appelle	
Ils	tu?	Elle	s'	appelle	

Look at the pictures and answer the questions below.

1 Who is talking to Anthony? Matteo

2 Who is playing basketball? luke

3 What is the lady called? Lucy

4 Who is leaving? Germain

Write your replies to the questions below in French.

Bonjour!

Je m'appelle cooper

ca va bien, merci.

Au revoir

Numbers

Les nombres

Here are the numbers from 1 to 20 in French.

1	**un**	6	**six**	11	**onze**	16	**seize**
2	**deux**	7	**sept**	12	**douze**	17	**dix-sept**
3	**trois**	8	**huit**	13	**treize**	18	**dix-huit**
4	**quatre**	9	**neuf**	14	**quatorze**	19	**dix-neuf**
5	**cinq**	10	**dix**	15	**quinze**	20	**vingt**

Write the number of items in French in each box.

 → quatre | six ← 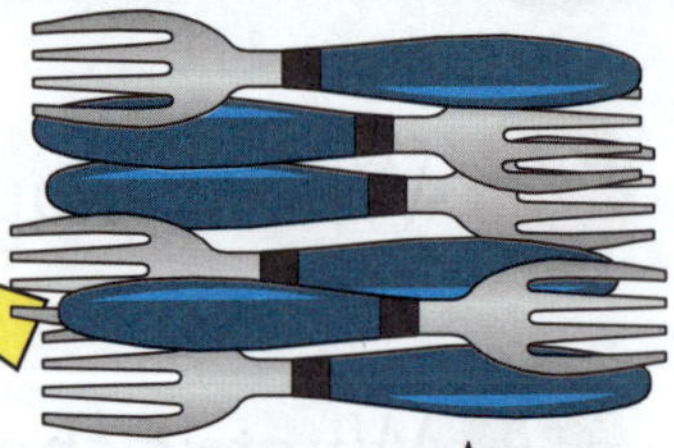

 → cinq | dix ← 

 → onze | treize ← 

Write the answers to these sums in numbers.

neuf + sept = 16

huit + trois = onze

onze + quatre = quinze

quatre + quatorze = dix-huit

vingt – sept = treize

dix-neuf – deux = dix-sept

Quel âge as-tu?
How old are you?

J'ai huit ans.
I'm eight years old.

Il a seize ans.
He is sixteen years old.

Elle a dix-neuf ans.
She is nineteen years old.

Write how old each person below is in French.

Il a quatre ans.

Il a donze ans

elle a dix sept ans

elle a sept ans

elle a onze ans

Il a neuf ans

Write your reply to the question below in French.

Quel âge as-tu?

J'ai huit ans

Colours

Les couleurs

Find the French words for colours in the word search.

c	i	a	j	d	m	e	b	c	g	m	e
g	b	i	e	c	o	l	o	u	r	s	d
e	l	h	d	b	d	l	e	v	j	a	n
f	e	l	g	p	j	k	h	n	e	o	h
r	u	i	b	l	a	n	c	f	r	r	e
p	o	f	j	e	u	e	m	a	g	n	t
d	e	u	h	n	n	j	c	h	g	o	e
n	a	e	g	k	e	d	i	s	b	i	t
c	f	i	m	e	c	o	a	e	p	r	h

~~white~~ black
~~blue~~ ~~green~~
~~yellow~~ red

Count how many balloons there are of each colour and write the number in French.

bleu trois

vert ~~cat~~ quatre

rouge six

jaune un

blanc deux

rose

orange

violet

marron

Complete the crossword below with the correct French words.

across
1 brown
2 blue
3 pink
4 purple

down
1 red
2 black
3 green

Write down what colour each item is in French.

Days and months

Les jours et les mois

Here are the days of the week in French.

lundi	Monday	**vendredi**	Friday
mardi	Tuesday	**samedi**	Saturday
mercredi	Wednesday	**dimanche**	Sunday
jeudi	Thursday		

Unscramble these French words to spell out days of the week.

a d i m n e c h → dimanche

r e v i d d e n → ....

r r e e m c d i → ....

a m s d i e → ....

n i d l u → ....

Complete the crossword below with the correct French words.

1 down: s a m e d i

2 across: m . . . .

across

1 The day before Monday.

2 The day after Tuesday.

down

1 Saturday

2 The day after Monday.

3 The day before Friday.

Here are the months of the year in French.

janvier January	**février** February	**mars** March	**avril** April	**mai** May	**juin** June	**juillet** July
août August	**septembre** September	**octobre** October	**novembre** November	**décembre** December		

Fill in the blanks to spell the French words below.

Remember!
In French, days of the week and months of the year don't need capital letters.

d ___ ___ ___ m ___ r ___

a ___ ___ t

___ c t ___ ___ ___ ___

___ a ___

___ u ___ l ___ ___ ___

___ v ___ ___ ___

The characters below are showing their birthday months. Write down the order in which their birthdays happen.

1 Clément

2 ....

3 ....

4 ....

5 ....

My family

Ma famille

Remember!

The word for 'my' changes depending on whether the following word is male or female. If the word is female, use 'ma', and if the word is male, use 'mon'.

Read the speech bubbles below and finish the sentences.

Lucas's father is called David

Lucas's mother is called Marina

Lucas's grandmother is called Elsa

Lucas's sister is called Holly

Lucas's grandfather is called Sid

Lucas's brother is called marco

Tu as des frères ou des sœurs?
Do you have any brothers or sisters?

Oui, j'ai un frère.
Yes, I have one brother.

Non, je suis fille unique.
No, I'm an only child. (girl)

Non, je suis fils unique.
No, I'm an only child. (boy)

Write each name next to the brothers and sisters they have.

1. Monica a deux frères.
2. Joey a une sœur et un frère.
3. Lily a trois sœurs.
4. David a une sœur.

David

Monica

Joey

Lily

Draw a line to match each French sentence to the correct English sentence.

J'ai une sœur et deux frères.	I have a brother and a sister.
Je suis fille unique.	I have one brother.
J'ai un frère.	I'm an only child. (girl)
Je suis fils unique.	I have one sister and two brothers.
J'ai un frère et une sœur.	I'm an only child. (boy)

My house

Chez moi

J'habite...
I live...

dans une maison
in a house

dans un appartement
in a flat

dans un château
in a castle

en ville
in the city

à la campagne
in the countryside

au bord de la mer
by the sea

Fill in the blanks below to show where each character lives.

J'habite ln ville.

J'habite dans un chateau

J'habite à la campagne.

J'habite au bord de la mer.

Practise and Learn

French

Ages 7-9

Answers

This section shows each of the pages from the book with the answers filled out.

The pages are laid out in the same way as the book itself, so the questions can be easily marked by you, or by your child.

There are also helpful learning tips with some of the pages.

4

Hello!

Bonjour!

bonsoir good evening
bonne nuit good night
à bientôt see you soon
pas mal not bad
très bien very well
pas très bien not very well

Fill in the gaps below to make a phrase for each picture.

Remember! 'Bonne nuit' is what you'd say before going to bed — just like 'good night'.

b o n n e   n u i t

b o n s o i r

p a s   t r è s   b i e n

a u   r e v o i r

4

5

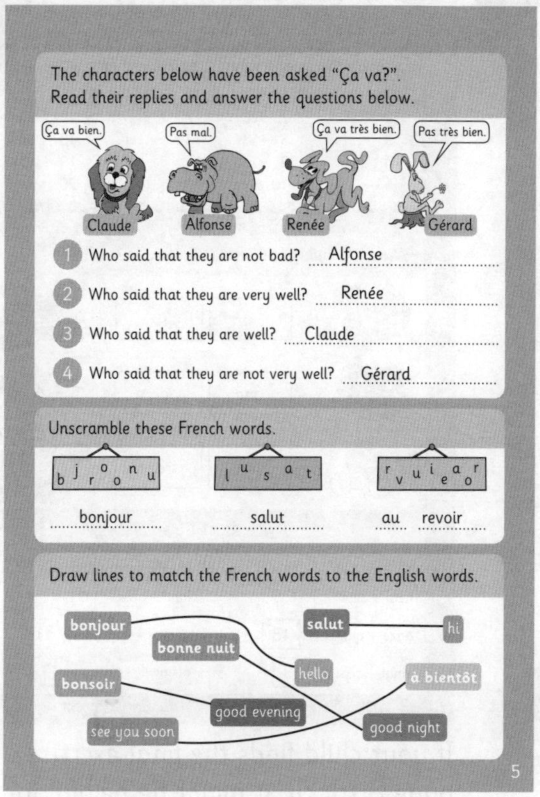

The characters below have been asked "Ça va?". Read their replies and answer the questions below.

1. Who said that they are not bad? Alfonse
2. Who said that they are very well? Renée
3. Who said that they are well? Claude
4. Who said that they are not very well? Gérard

Unscramble these French words.

b j r o o n u — bonjour

l u s a t — salut

r v u i e a o r — au revoir

Draw lines to match the French words to the English words.

bonjour — hello
salut — hi
bonne nuit — good night
bonsoir — good evening
à bientôt — see you soon

5

6

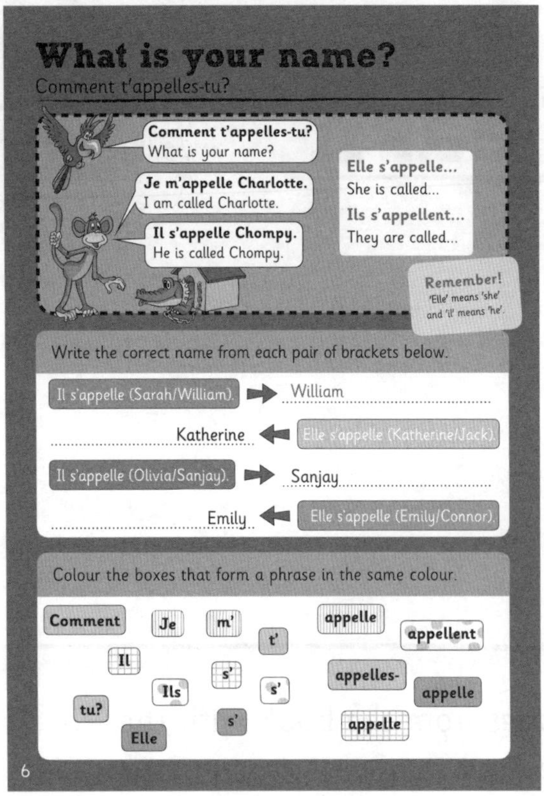

What is your name?

Comment t'appelles-tu?

Comment t'appelles-tu? What is your name?

Je m'appelle Charlotte. I am called Charlotte.

Il s'appelle Chompy. He is called Chompy.

Elle s'appelle... She is called...

Ils s'appellent... They are called...

Remember! 'Elle' means 'she' and 'il' means 'he'.

Write the correct name from each pair of brackets below.

Il s'appelle (Sarah/William). → William

Katherine ← Elle s'appelle (Katherine/Jack).

Il s'appelle (Olivia/Sanjay). → Sanjay

Emily ← Elle s'appelle (Emily/Connor).

Colour the boxes that form a phrase in the same colour.

Comment | Je | m' | t' | appelle | appellent | Il | s' | Ils | s' | appelles- | appelle | tu? | s' | Elle | appelle

6

7

Look at the pictures and answer the questions below.

1 Who is talking to Anthony? Matteo

2 Who is playing basketball? Luke

3 What is the lady called? Lucy

4 Who is leaving? Germain

Write your replies to the questions below in French.

Bonjour! — Bonjour!

Comment t'appelles-tu? — Je m'appelle (your name).

Ça va? — Ça va bien / très bien / pas très bien.

Au revoir! — Au revoir!

VARIOUS ANSWERS POSSIBLE

7

There is more than one possible response to 'Ça va?'. Encourage your child to give different replies each time you ask 'Ça va?'.

8

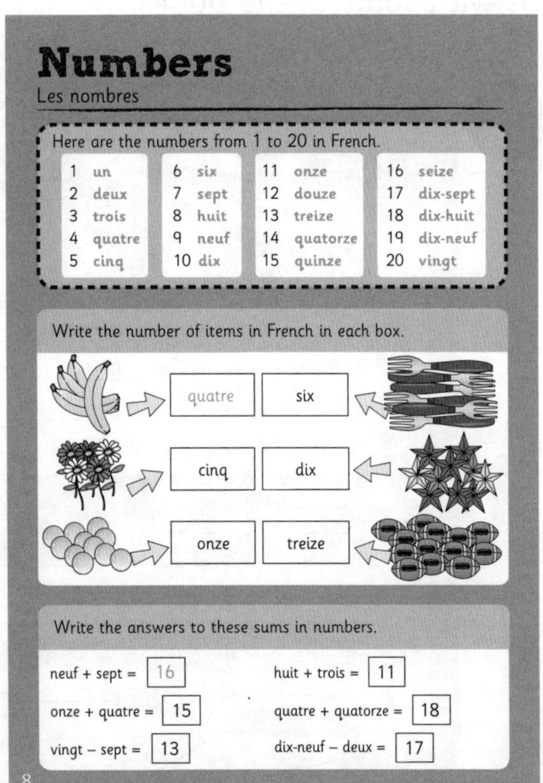

Numbers

Les nombres

Here are the numbers from 1 to 20 in French.

1	un	6	six	11	onze	16	seize
2	deux	7	sept	12	douze	17	dix-sept
3	trois	8	huit	13	treize	18	dix-huit
4	quatre	9	neuf	14	quatorze	19	dix-neuf
5	cinq	10	dix	15	quinze	20	vingt

Write the number of items in French in each box.

quatre | six

cinq | dix

onze | treize

Write the answers to these sums in numbers.

neuf + sept = 16

huit + trois = 11

onze + quatre = 15

quatre + quatorze = 18

vingt − sept = 13

dix-neuf − deux = 17

8

If your child finds the final exercise on page 8 tricky, it might be helpful for them to translate the sums into English before working out the answer.

9

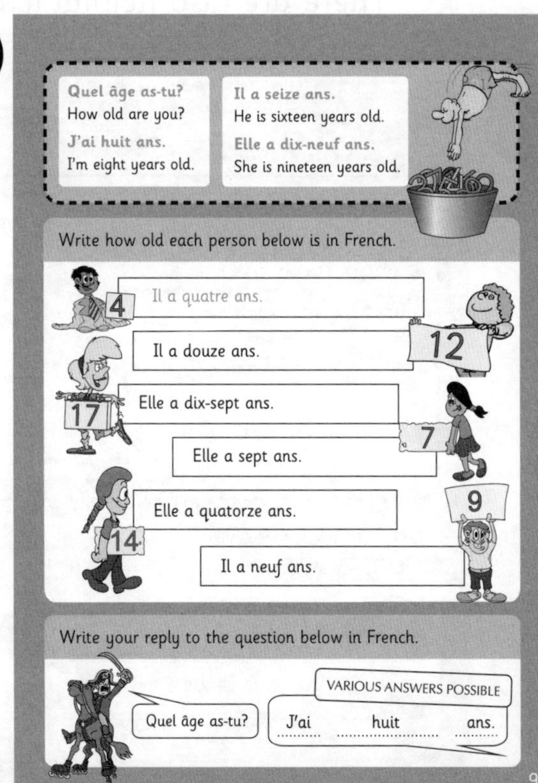

Quel âge as-tu? How old are you?

J'ai huit ans. I'm eight years old.

Il a seize ans. He is sixteen years old.

Elle a dix-neuf ans. She is nineteen years old.

Write how old each person below is in French.

4 — Il a quatre ans.

12 — Il a douze ans.

17 — Elle a dix-sept ans.

7 — Elle a sept ans.

14 — Elle a quatorze ans.

9 — Il a neuf ans.

Write your reply to the question below in French.

Quel âge as-tu? — J'ai huit ans.

VARIOUS ANSWERS POSSIBLE

9

10

Colours

Les couleurs

rouge · vert · blanc · bleu · jaune · noir

Find the French words for colours in the word search.

c	i	a	j	d	m	e	b	c	g	m	e
g	b	i	e	c	o	l	o	u	r	s	d
e	l	h	d	b	d	l	e	v	j	a	n
f	e	l	g	p	j	k	h	n	e	o	h
r	u	i	b	l	a	n	c	f	r	r	e
p	o	f	j	e	u	e	m	a	g	n	t
d	e	u	h	n	n	j	c	h	g	o	e
n	a	e	g	k	e	d	i	s	b	i	t
c	f	i	m	e	c	o	a	e	p	r	h

~~white~~ black
blue green
yellow red

Count how many balloons there are of each colour and write the number in French.

bleu trois
vert quatre
rouge six
jaune un
blanc deux

10

11

rose · orange · violet · marron

Complete the crossword below with the correct French words.

across
1 brown
~~2 blue~~
3 pink
4 purple

down
1 red
2 black
3 green

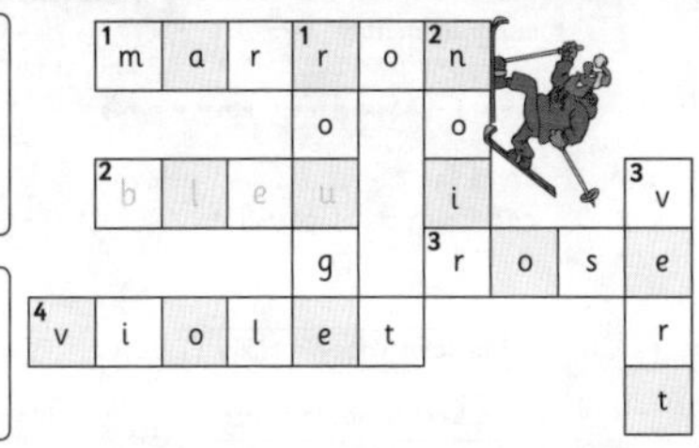

Write down what colour each item is in French.

rouge · rose · marron · jaune · bleu

11

Encourage your child to point to items around the house and say what colour they are in French.

12

Days and months

Les jours et les mois

Here are the days of the week in French.

lundi	Monday	vendredi	Friday
mardi	Tuesday	samedi	Saturday
mercredi	Wednesday	dimanche	Sunday
jeudi	Thursday		

Unscramble these French words to spell out days of the week.

a d i m n e c h → dimanche
r e v i d d e n → vendredi
r r e e m c d i → mercredi
a m s d i e → samedi
n i d l u → lundi

Complete the crossword below with the correct French words.

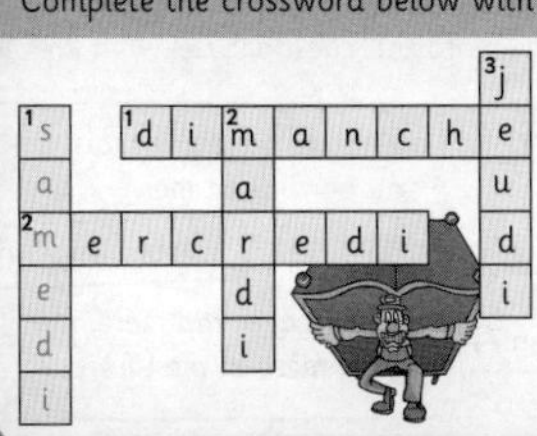

across
1 The day before Monday.
2 The day after Tuesday.

down
~~1 Saturday~~
2 The day after Monday.
3 The day before Friday.

12

To help your child remember the French days and months, you could write them alongside the English words on a calendar or timetable.

13

Here are the months of the year in French.

janvier January	février February	mars March	avril April	mai May	juin June	juillet July
août August	septembre September	octobre October	novembre November	décembre December		

Fill in the blanks to spell the French words below.

Remember! In French, days of the week and months of the year don't need capital letters.

d é c e m b r e · a o û t
o c t o b r e · m a i
j u i l l e t · a v r i l

The characters below are showing their birthday months. Write down the order in which their birthdays happen.

1 Clément
2 Guillaume
3 Antoine
4 Olivier
5 Étienne

13

You could extend the last exercise on page 13 by asking your child to write down the months of their friends' birthdays in French.

14

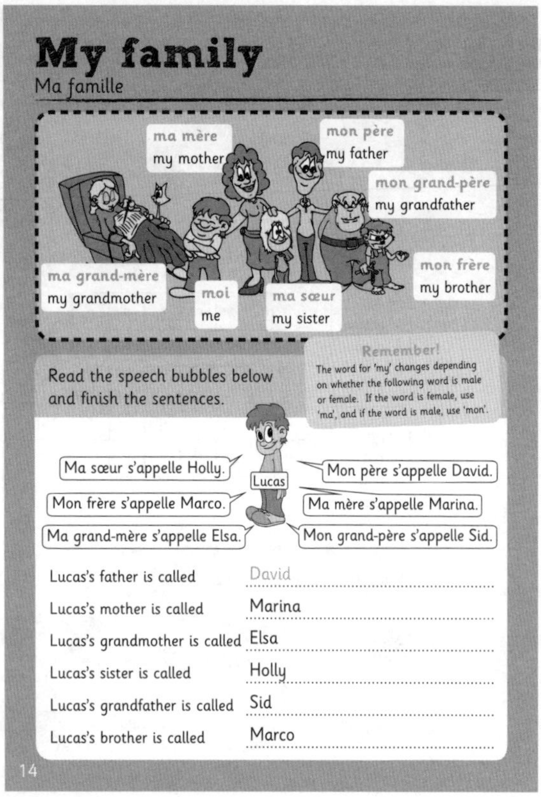

My family
Ma famille

Read the speech bubbles below and finish the sentences.

Remember! The word for 'my' changes depending on whether the following word is male or female. If the word is female, use 'ma', and if the word is male, use 'mon'.

Lucas's father is called David

Lucas's mother is called Marina

Lucas's grandmother is called Elsa

Lucas's sister is called Holly

Lucas's grandfather is called Sid

Lucas's brother is called Marco

14

As an extension, you could ask your child to write about their family, or a family from their favourite TV programme.

15

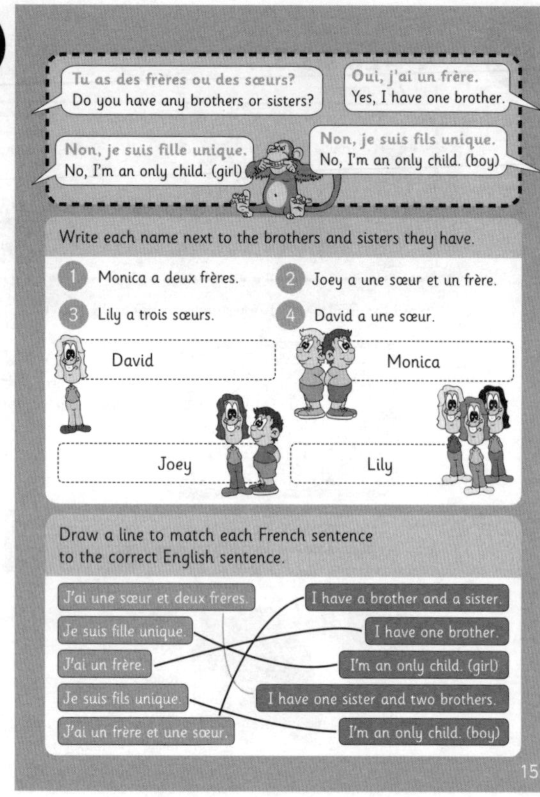

Write each name next to the brothers and sisters they have.

1. Monica a deux frères.
2. Joey a une sœur et un frère.
3. Lily a trois sœurs.
4. David a une sœur.

David — Monica — Joey — Lily

Draw a line to match each French sentence to the correct English sentence.

J'ai une sœur et deux frères.	I have a brother and a sister.
Je suis fille unique.	I have one brother.
J'ai un frère.	I'm an only child. (girl)
Je suis fils unique.	I have one sister and two brothers.
J'ai un frère et une sœur.	I'm an only child. (boy)

15

For extra practice, you could ask your child to write about the ages of family members, using French vocabulary from page 9.

16

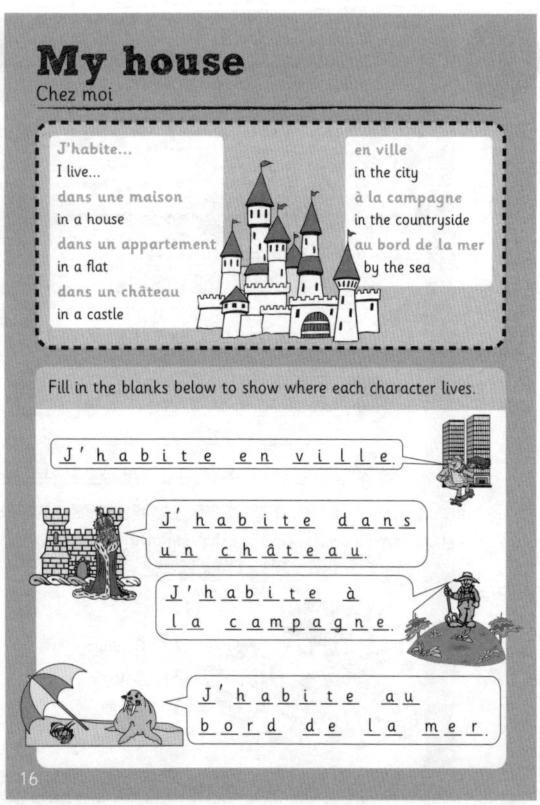

My house
Chez moi

Fill in the blanks below to show where each character lives.

J'habite en ville.

J'habite dans un château.

J'habite à la campagne.

J'habite au bord de la mer.

16

17

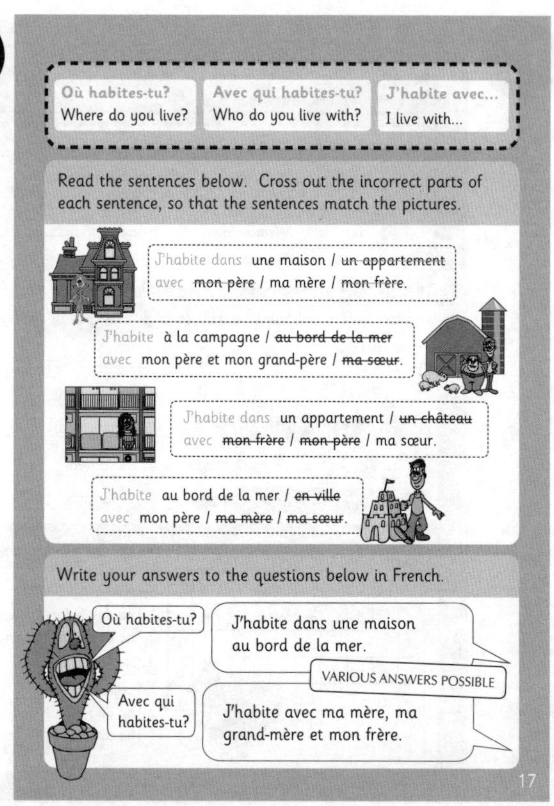

Read the sentences below. Cross out the incorrect parts of each sentence, so that the sentences match the pictures.

J'habite dans une maison / ~~un appartement~~ avec ~~mon père~~ / ma mère / ~~mon frère~~.

J'habite à la campagne / ~~au bord de la mer~~ avec mon père et mon grand-père / ~~ma sœur~~.

J'habite dans un appartement / ~~un château~~ avec ~~mon frère~~ / ~~mon père~~ / ma sœur.

J'habite au bord de la mer / ~~en ville~~ avec mon père / ~~ma mère~~ / ~~ma sœur~~.

Write your answers to the questions below in French.

Où habites-tu? — J'habite dans une maison au bord de la mer.

VARIOUS ANSWERS POSSIBLE

Avec qui habites-tu? — J'habite avec ma mère, ma grand-mère et mon frère.

17

18

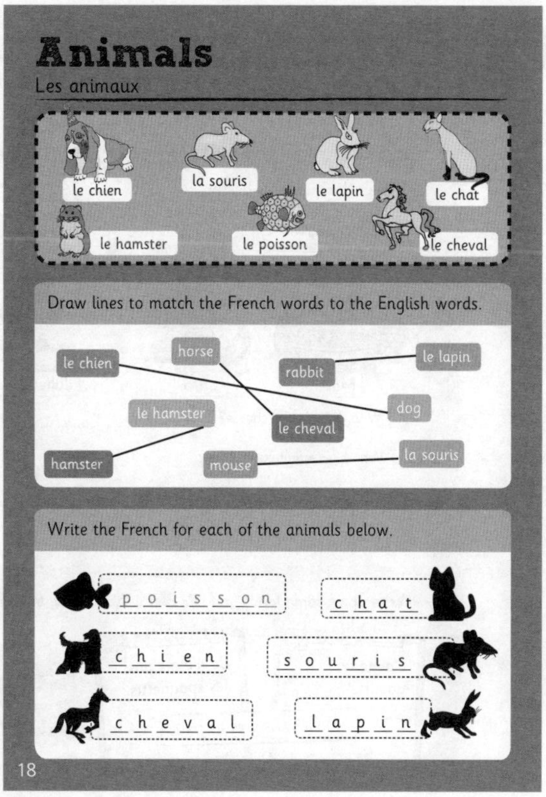

Animals

Les animaux

le chien, la souris, le lapin, le chat, le hamster, le poisson, le cheval

Draw lines to match the French words to the English words.

le chien – dog; horse – le cheval; rabbit – le lapin; le hamster – hamster; mouse – la souris

Write the French for each of the animals below.

p o i s s o n

c h a t

c h i e n

s o u r i s

c h e v a l

l a p i n

18

19

le serpent, l'oiseau, la tortue, l'araignée

As-tu un animal?
Do you have a pet?
Oui, j'ai...
Yes, I have...
Non, je n'ai pas d'animaux.
No, I don't have any pets.

Three people were asked "As-tu un animal?". Write down the answer they would give in French.

Remember! To say 'a' or 'one' you need to use 'un' for masculine words and 'une' for feminine words.

Oui, j'ai un chien et un serpent.

Oui, j'ai deux hamsters.

Oui, j'ai deux tortues et un chat.

Circle either 'True' or 'False' for each statement below.

J'ai un chien, deux araignées, un serpent, un oiseau et deux souris.

1. He has no mice. True / (False)
2. He has one snake. (True) / False
3. He has more dogs than spiders. True / (False)
4. He has more mice than birds. (True) / False

19

If your child finds the final exercise tricky, it may be helpful for them to translate the speech bubble into English, before answering the questions.

20

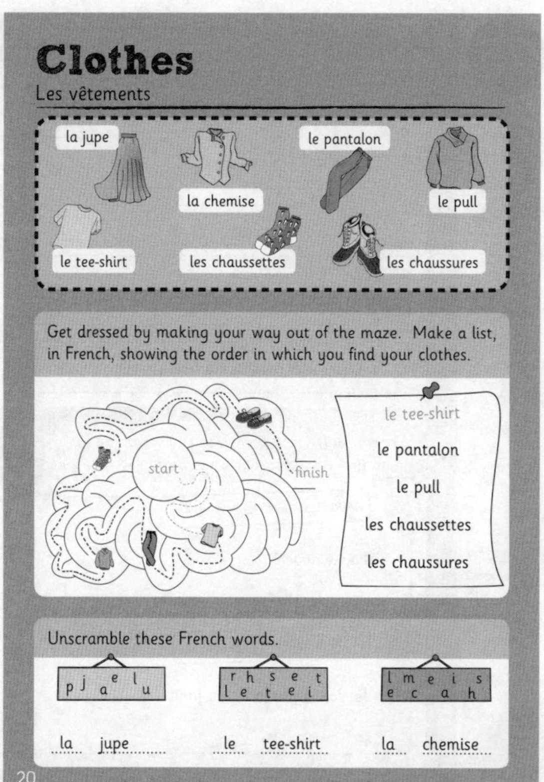

Clothes

Les vêtements

la jupe, la chemise, le pantalon, le pull, le tee-shirt, les chaussettes, les chaussures

Get dressed by making your way out of the maze. Make a list, in French, showing the order in which you find your clothes.

start – finish

le tee-shirt
le pantalon
le pull
les chaussettes
les chaussures

Unscramble these French words.

p j a e l u – la jupe

r h s e t l e t e i – le tee-shirt

l m e i s e c a h – la chemise

20

21

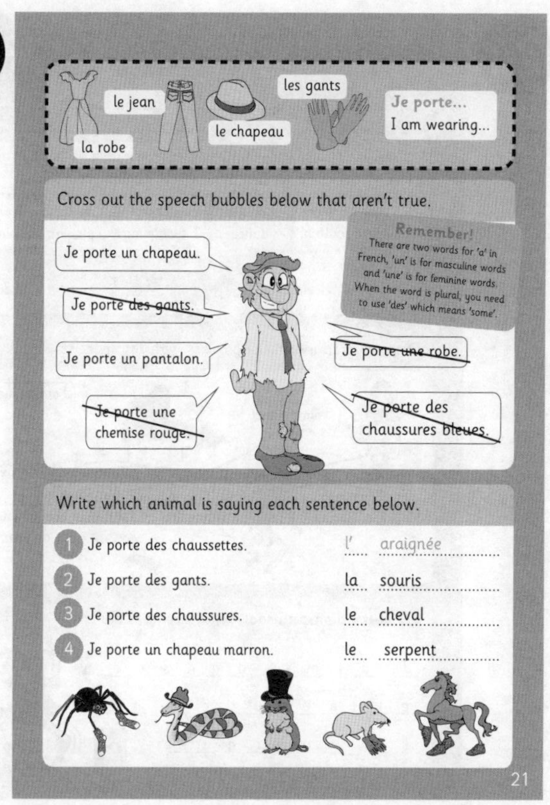

la robe, le jean, le chapeau, les gants

Je porte...
I am wearing...

Cross out the speech bubbles below that aren't true.

Remember! There are two words for 'a' in French, 'un' is for masculine words and 'une' is for feminine words. When the word is plural, you need to use 'des' which means 'some'.

Je porte un chapeau.

~~Je porte des gants.~~

Je porte un pantalon.

~~Je porte une chemise rouge.~~

~~Je porte une robe.~~

~~Je porte des chaussures bleues.~~

Write which animal is saying each sentence below.

1. Je porte des chaussettes. l' araignée
2. Je porte des gants. la souris
3. Je porte des chaussures. le cheval
4. Je porte un chapeau marron. le serpent

21

22

Food

La nourriture

le pain | les frites | le sandwich | le jambon | le fromage
la pomme | le chocolat | la pizza | les spaghettis | le yaourt

Complete the crossword below with the correct French words.

across	down
1. chips	1. cheese
2. ham	2. sandwich
3. bread	
4. apple	

				[1] f	r	i	t	e	[2] s
				r					a
[2] j	a	m	b	o	n				n
				m					d
			[3] p	a	i	n			w
				g					i
[4] p	o	m	m	e					c
									h

22

23

J'aime... I like...

Je n'aime pas... I don't like...

Answer the questions below.

Marc: J'aime les spaghettis. Je n'aime pas le pain.

Enzo: Je n'aime pas la pizza. J'aime les frites.

Juliette: Je n'aime pas le fromage. J'aime le chocolat.

1. Who doesn't like cheese? Juliette
2. Who likes spaghetti? Marc
3. Who doesn't like pizza? Enzo
4. Who doesn't like bread? Marc

Write down some foods you like and dislike below, in French.

J'aime le yaourt.

Je n'aime pas les spaghettis.

VARIOUS ANSWERS POSSIBLE

Remember! Start your sentences with either 'J'aime' or 'Je n'aime pas' and remember to include either 'le' or 'la' for each item of food.

23

24

What do you like doing?

Qu'est-ce que tu aimes faire?

J'aime... I like...
Je n'aime pas... I don't like...
...écouter de la musique ...listening to music
...jouer au foot ...playing football
...danser ...dancing
...nager ...swimming
...jouer du piano ...playing the piano
...regarder la télé ...watching television
...lire ...reading

Draw lines to match the pictures with the speech bubbles.

J'aime nager.

J'aime jouer du piano.

J'aime danser.

J'aime lire.

J'aime jouer au foot.

Fill in the blanks to show what Lee likes doing.

J'aime danser et écouter de la musique.

24

Make sure your child remembers to add accents to letters where needed, e.g. 'é' and that they are drawn in the right direction.

25

For each picture below, write a sentence to show whether each character likes or doesn't like what they're doing.

Je n'aime pas nager.

J'aime danser.

J'aime lire.

Je n'aime pas regarder la télé.

Write a sentence in French to say what you like doing and what you don't like doing.

VARIOUS ANSWERS POSSIBLE

J'aime nager.

VARIOUS ANSWERS POSSIBLE

Je n'aime pas jouer au foot.

25

26

What time is it?

Quelle heure est-il?

Quelle heure est-il? What time is it?	**À dix heures...** At ten o'clock...	**...du matin** ...in the morning
Il est deux heures. It's two o'clock.		**...du soir** ...in the evening

Draw a line to match each French sentence to the correct English sentence.

- It's three o'clock. — **Il est trois heures.**
- **Il est dix heures du matin.** — It's ten o'clock in the morning.
- It's six o'clock in the evening. — **Il est six heures du soir.**
- It's one o'clock. — **Il est une heure.**

Write down the time using answers from the box.

Quelle heure est-il?

~~Il est neuf heures du matin.~~	Il est quatre heures du matin.
Il est huit heures du soir.	Il est cinq heures du soir.

1. 9 am Il est neuf heures du matin.
2. 5 pm Il est cinq heures du soir.
3. 8 pm Il est huit heures du soir.
4. 4 am Il est quatre heures du matin.

26

It might be helpful for your child to look back at the page on 'Numbers' (page 8) to help with these exercises.

27

Write what time it is in French for each picture below.

- Il est trois heures.
- Il est sept heures.
- Il est dix heures.
- Il est deux heures.
- Il est onze heures.

Read what Louis is saying about his hobbies, then answer the questions below in English.

Je joue au foot à dix heures. Je regarde la télé à onze heures. J'écoute de la musique à trois heures.

Louis

At what time does Louis play football? 10 o'clock

At what time does Louis watch television? 11 o'clock

At what time does Louis listen to music? 3 o'clock

27

28

In my town

Dans ma ville

l'école school	**les magasins** shops
la piscine swimming pool	**la gare** train station
le café coffee shop	**la bibliothèque** library

Colour in the correct spelling of each French word.

la gare	la garre	les magasins	les magasines
lecolle	l'école	la bibliothèque	la biblioteck
la piesine	la piscine	le caffe	le café

Circle either 'true' or 'false' for each statement below.

Dans ma ville, il y a deux cafés, une piscine, une école, une gare et des magasins.

Remember! 'il y a' means 'there are'.

1. There is a school in his town. (True) / False
2. There are two swimming pools. True / (False)
3. There are no shops. True / (False)
4. There are two coffee shops. (True) / False

28

29

Find the French words for buildings in the word search below.

b	l	e	y	p	v	a	l	u	i	o	k
i	d	k	l	n	é	u	q	h	h	g	t
b	t	m	w	f	c	j	e	n	v	a	c
l	e	p	a	y	o	c	p	o	g	r	v
i	a	c	l	g	f	n	i	h	b	e	l
o	s	l	m	d	a	v	s	q	u	k	w
t	o	e	q	o	j	s	c	g	i	h	z
h	l	m	z	u	t	w	i	v	a	k	m
è	é	c	o	l	e	t	n	n	v	b	h
q	g	o	h	k	m	g	e	t	s	d	u
u	d	b	m	a	t	t	e	o	h	é	f
e	p	g	h	e	e	e	a	g	y	a	a

school
swimming pool
coffee shop
shops
train station
library

The map below shows Sam's trip through town. Write down the order in which he visits each building during his trip.

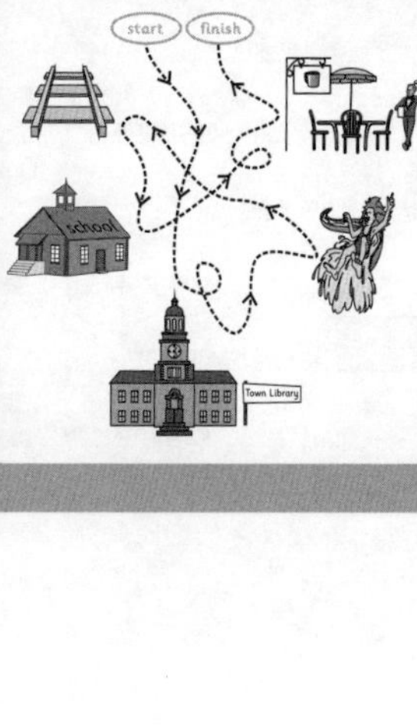

1. la bibliothèque
2. la piscine
3. la gare
4. l'école
5. le café

29

30

Masculine and feminine

All things in French are either masculine or feminine. The French words for 'the', 'a' and 'my' change depending on whether the word that follows is masculine or feminine.

feminine	masculine
la **chemise** the shirt	le **pull** the jumper
une **chemise** a shirt	un **pull** a jumper
ma **chemise** my shirt	mon **pull** my jumper

Add 'mon' or 'ma' to each of these family members.

1 ma grand-mère
2 mon grand-père
3 mon père
4 mon frère
5 ma mère
6 ma sœur

Leo has confused his masculines and feminines. Rewrite what he has said with 'un', 'une', 'le' and 'la' in the right places.

Je porte un chemise et une pantalon. J'ai une chat. J'aime la fromage et la jambon.

Je porte une chemise et un pantalon. J'ai un chat. J'aime le fromage et le jambon.

30

31

Write the French words for the items below on the correct clipboard.

masculine	feminine
le jean	la pomme
le pain	la pizza
le chapeau	la jupe
le poisson	

Look at the words below. Work out if they are masculine or feminine. Write 'm' in the boxes for the masculine ones, and 'f' in the boxes for the feminine ones.

- **la fleur** f
- **le cadeau** m
- **le bateau** m
- **une glace** f
- **ma voiture** f
- **un stylo** m
- **ma banane** f
- **mon couteau** m

31

Grammar is often tricky, so it might be helpful to read the teaching boxes on these pages with your child, to make sure that they understand them.

32

Plurals

If there's more than one of something, you need to add an 's' to the end of the word (unless there already is an 's').

une pomme deux pommes one apple two apples

une souris deux souris one mouse two mice

masculine	feminine
le **chat** the cat	la **jupe** the skirt
les **chats** the cats	les **jupes** the skirts
mes **chats** my cats	mes **jupes** my skirts
des **chats** some cats	des **jupes** some skirts

Remember! The words for 'the', 'my', and 'some' are the same for masculine and feminine words when you talk about more than one of something.

Write these plural phrases in French on the lines below.

- my sisters → mes sœurs
- some shoes → des chaussures
- some skirts → des jupes
- my chips → mes frites
- the apples → les pommes
- the dogs → les chiens

FP4Q21

32

Où habites-tu?
Where do you live?

Avec qui habites-tu?
Who do you live with?

J'habite avec...
I live with...

Read the sentences below. Cross out the incorrect parts of each sentence, so that the sentences match the pictures.

J'habite dans une maison / un appartement
avec mon père / ma mère / mon frère.

J'habite à la campagne / au bord de la mer
avec mon père et mon grand-père / ma sœur.

J'habite dans un appartement / un château
avec mon frère / mon père / ma sœur.

J'habite au bord de la mer / en ville
avec mon père / ma mère / ma sœur.

Write your answers to the questions below in French.

Où habites-tu?

J'habite dans une maison avec ma famille

Avec qui habites-tu?

Animals

Les animaux

Draw lines to match the French words to the English words.

le chien — horse — rabbit — le lapin

le hamster — le cheval — dog

hamster — mouse — la souris

Write the French for each of the animals below.

p o i s s o n

chat

chien

soucis

cheval

lapin

le serpent

l'oiseau

la tortue

l'araignée

As-tu un animal?
Do you have a pet?
Oui, j'ai...
Yes, I have...
Non, je n'ai pas d'animaux.
No, I don't have any pets.

Three people were asked "As-tu un animal?". Write down the answer they would give in French.

Remember!
To say 'a' or 'one' you need to use 'un' for masculine words and 'une' for feminine words.

Oui, j'ai un chien et un serpent.

Oui, j'ai deux chi souris un

oui j'ai un chat et deux tortue.

Circle either 'True' or 'False' for each statement below.

J'ai un chien, deux araignées, un serpent, un oiseau et deux souris.

1. He has no mice. True / (False)
2. He has one snake. (True) / False
3. He has more dogs than spiders. (True) / False
4. He has more mice than birds. (True) / False

Clothes

Les vêtements

Get dressed by making your way out of the maze. Make a list, in French, showing the order in which you find your clothes.

le tee-shirt
le pantalon
le pull
les chaussettes
les chaussures

Unscramble these French words.

p j e l a u

r h s e t l e t e i

l m e i s e c a h

la jupe .... les chaussettes .... la chemise ....

Je porte...
I am wearing...

Cross out the speech bubbles below that aren't true.

Remember!
There are two words for 'a' in French, 'un' is for masculine words and 'une' is for feminine words. When the word is plural, you need to use 'des' which means 'some'.

Write which animal is saying each sentence below.

1. Je porte des chaussettes. l' araignée
2. Je porte des gants. la Souris
3. Je porte des chaussures. le Cheval
4. Je porte un chapeau marron. le serpent

Food

La nourriture

le pain | les frites | le sandwich | le jambon | le fromage

la pomme | le chocolat | la pizza | les spaghettis | le yaourt

Complete the crossword below with the correct French words.

across	down
~~1. chips~~	1. cheese
2. ham	2. sandwich
3. bread	
4. apple	

J'aime...
I like...

Je n'aime pas...
I don't like...

Answer the questions below.

J'aime les spaghettis.
Je n'aime pas le pain.

Je n'aime pas la pizza.
J'aime les frites.

Je n'aime pas le fromage.
J'aime le chocolat.

Marc

Enzo

Juliette

1. Who doesn't like cheese? Juliette ....
2. Who likes spaghetti? ....
3. Who doesn't like pizza? ....
4. Who doesn't like bread? ....

Write down some foods you like and dislike below, in French.

Remember!
Start your sentences with either 'J'aime' or 'Je n'aime pas' and remember to include either 'le' or 'la' for each item of food.

What do you like doing?

Qu'est-ce que tu aimes faire?

J'aime...
I like...

Je n'aime pas...
I don't like...

...écouter de la musique
...listening to music

...jouer au foot
...playing football

...danser
...dancing

...nager
...swimming

...jouer du piano
...playing the piano

...regarder la télé
...watching television

...lire
...reading

Draw lines to match the pictures with the speech bubbles.

J'aime nager.

J'aime jouer du piano.

J'aime danser.

J'aime lire.

J'aime jouer au foot.

Fill in the blanks to show what Lee likes doing.

J' _ _ _ _ d _ _ _ _

e t _ c _ _ _ _ r _ e

_ _ _ _ s _ _ _ _ _.

For each picture below, write a sentence to show whether each character likes or doesn't like what they're doing.

Je n'aime pas nager.

Write a sentence in French to say what you like doing and what you don't like doing.

What time is it?

Quelle heure est-il?

Quelle heure est-il?
What time is it?

Il est deux heures.
It's two o'clock.

À dix heures...
At ten o'clock...

...du matin
...in the morning

...du soir
...in the evening

Draw a line to match each French sentence to the correct English sentence.

It's three o'clock.	**Il est dix heures du matin.**
Il est trois heures.	It's six o'clock in the evening.
Il est six heures du soir.	It's one o'clock.
Il est une heure.	It's ten o'clock in the morning.

Write down the time using answers from the box.

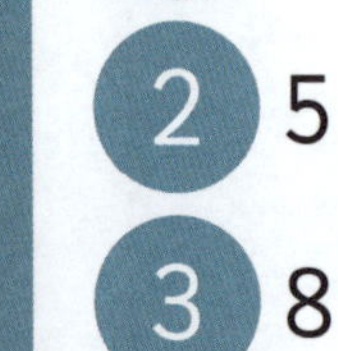

Quelle heure est-il?

~~**Il est neuf heures du matin.**~~	**Il est quatre heures du matin.**
Il est huit heures du soir.	**Il est cinq heures du soir.**

1 9 am Il est neuf heures du matin. ....

2 5 pm ....

3 8 pm ....

4 4 am ....

Write what time it is in French for each picture below.

Il est trois heures.

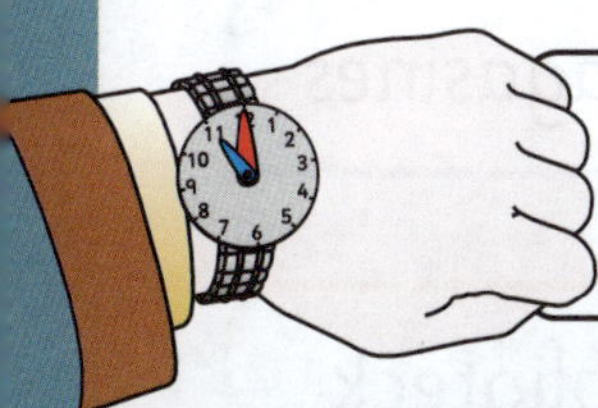

Read what Louis is saying about his hobbies, then answer the questions below in English.

Je joue au foot à dix heures. Je regarde la télé à onze heures. J'écoute de la musique à trois heures.

At what time does Louis play football? ....

At what time does Louis watch television? ....

At what time does Louis listen to music? ....

In my town

Dans ma ville

l'école
school

la piscine
swimming pool

le café
coffee shop

les magasins
shops

la gare
train station

la bibliothèque
library

Colour in the correct spelling of each French word.

la gare	la garre
les magasins	les magasines
lecolle	l'école
la bibliothèque	la biblioteck
la piesine	la piscine
le caffe	le café

Circle either 'true' or 'false' for each statement below.

Dans ma ville, il y a deux cafés, une piscine, une école, une gare et des magasins.

Remember! 'il y a' means 'there are'.

1. There is a school in his town. True / False
2. There are two swimming pools. True / False
3. There are no shops. True / False
4. There are two coffee shops. True / False

Find the French words for buildings in the word search below.

b	l	e	y	p	v	a	l	u	i	o	k
i	d	k	l	n	é	u	q	h	h	g	t
b	t	m	w	f	c	j	e	n	v	a	c
l	e	p	a	y	o	c	p	o	g	r	v
i	a	c	l	g	f	n	i	h	b	e	l
o	s	l	m	d	a	v	s	q	u	k	w
t	o	e	q	o	j	s	c	g	i	h	z
h	l	m	z	u	t	w	i	v	a	k	m
è	é	c	o	l	e	t	n	n	v	b	h
q	g	o	h	k	m	g	e	t	s	d	u
u	d	b	m	a	t	t	e	o	h	é	f
e	p	g	h	e	e	e	a	g	y	a	a

school
swimming pool
coffee shop
~~shops~~
train station
library

The map below shows Sam's trip through town. Write down the order in which he visits each building during his trip.

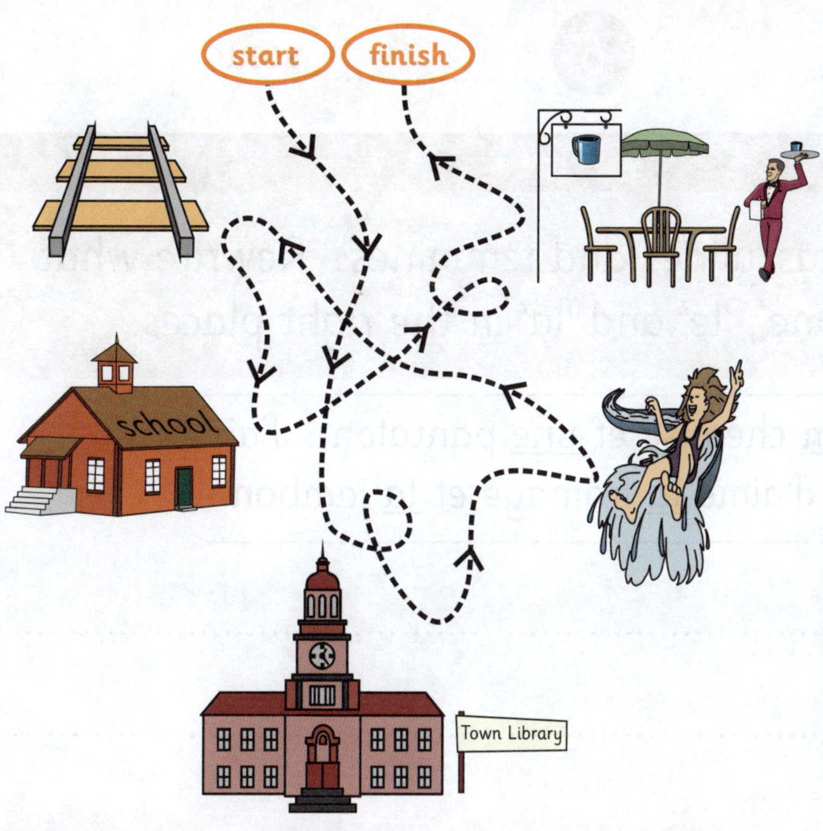

1. la bibliothèque
2.
3.
4.
5.

Masculine and feminine

All things in French are either masculine or feminine. The French words for 'the', 'a' and 'my' change depending on whether the word that follows is masculine or feminine.

feminine		masculine	
la chemise	the shirt	**le pull**	the jumper
une chemise	a shirt	**un pull**	a jumper
ma chemise	my shirt	**mon pull**	my jumper

Add 'mon' or 'ma' to each of these family members.

1 ma .... grand-mère

2 .... grand-père

3 .... père

4 .... frère

5 .... mère

6 .... sœur

Leo has confused his masculines and feminines. Rewrite what he has said with 'un', 'une', 'le' and 'la' in the right places.

Je porte un chemise et une pantalon. J'ai une chat. J'aime la fromage et la jambon.

....

....

....

Write the French words for the items below on the correct clipboard.

masculine

le jean

feminine

Look at the words below. Work out if they are masculine or feminine. Write 'm' in the boxes for the masculine ones, and 'f' in the boxes for the feminine ones.

la fleur

f

le cadeau

le bateau

une glace

ma voiture

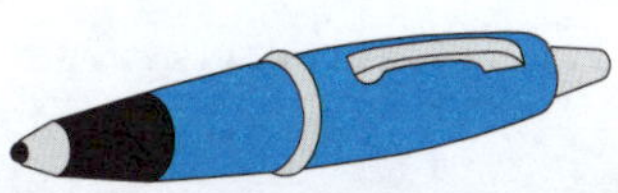

un stylo

ma banane

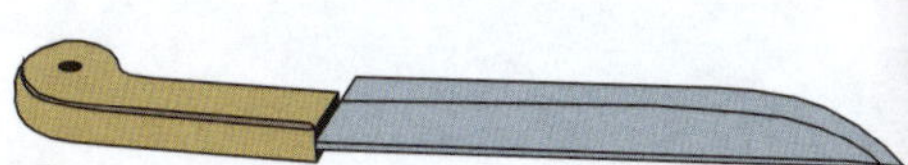

mon couteau

Plurals

If there's more than one of something, you need to add an 's' to the end of the word (unless there already is an 's').

une pomme	deux pommes
one apple	two apples

une souris	deux souris
one mouse	two mice

masculine	
le chat	the cat
les chats	the cats
mes chats	my cats
des chats	some cats

feminine	
la jupe	the skirt
les jupes	the skirts
mes jupes	my skirts
des jupes	some skirts

Remember!
The words for 'the', 'my', and 'some' are the same for masculine and feminine words when you talk about more than one of something.

Write these plural phrases in French on the lines below.

my sisters → mes sœurs ....

some shoes → ....

some skirts → ....

my chips → ....

the apples → ....

the dogs → ....

FP4Q22